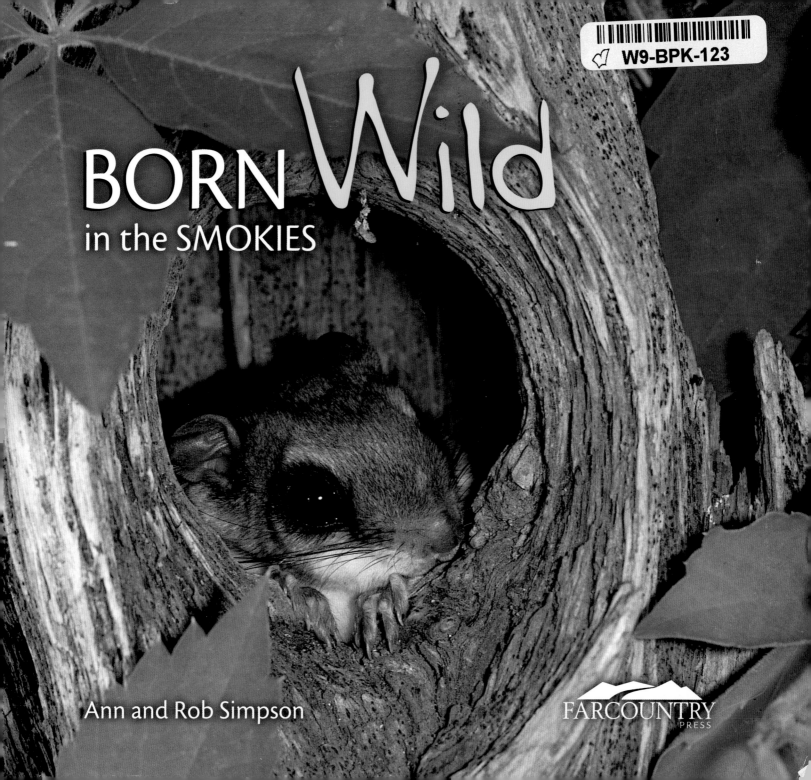

BORN Wild
in the SMOKIES

Ann and Rob Simpson

FARCOUNTRY
PRESS

Right: A white-tailed fawn is curled in a patch of green, hidden away from predators. After the doe feeds the fawn early in the morning, she hides the fawn and grazes nearby. If you happen on a fawn, do not disturb it, for the doe will return to fetch it.

Title page: Nestled in its burrow, this southern flying squirrel keeps an eye out for predators.

Cover: Under the watchful eye of its father, this bold fawn takes a stand among the flowers and grasses of Great Smoky Mountains National Park.

Back cover: This tiny black bear cub rests in the crook of a tree branch.

ISBN 10: 1-56037-415-2
ISBN 13: 978-1-56037-415-2

© 2007 by Farcountry Press
Photography © 2007 by Ann and Rob Simpson

For more information about our books, write Farcountry Press, P.O. Box 5630, Helena, MT 59604; call (800) 821-3874; or visit www.farcountrypress.com.

Created, produced, and designed in the United States.
Printed in China.

17   16   15   14   13   2   3   4   5   6

• INTRODUCTION •

Eastern box turtles are well known for their double-hinged shells, which allow them to completely retract their bodies into their protective covering.

• BY ANN & ROB SIMPSON •

As the warm spring sun slowly melts the winter snow, a doe makes a bed in the fresh meadow grass and lies down to give birth in a valley, nearly hidden by soft blankets of blue-tinged fog. Before the fawn's eyes have started to focus, it will begin to hear the gentle gurgle of a nearby stream, smell the earthy aroma of the blossoming woodlands, and feel the warmth of its mother and the rough kiss of her tongue. As days pass, the fawn settles in and grows up in the Appalachian Mountains of Tennessee and North Carolina, another of the many generations of animals born wild in the Smokies.

Not all wild animal births are as openly dramatic—salamanders hatch hidden under rocks, bear cubs are born during their mothers' deep winter slumber, and tadpoles emerge quietly under water—but all are part of the great tapestry of life in Great Smoky Mountains National Park. Most of the wild babies in this book were photographed in Great Smoky Mountains National Park—the rest were photographed in the area around the park.

Every springtime, as the sounds of returning birds fill the woods, this old story of renewal and birth begins again. The warming temperatures summon the return of neotropical migrant birds from their winter homes. Above the sound of the rushing waterways swollen with spring rain, the ringing song of Louisiana waterthrushes can be heard. Spring peepers, wood frogs, and eastern phoebes make melodious announcements of their arrivals. Male red-winged blackbirds raucously proclaim their territory while perched on wetland snags.

Although many of these creatures rush to define their territories to make sure that they stake out the best-suited areas to raise their young, there are disadvantages to these early arrivals. Occasionally spring is interrupted by a rogue cold front that blankets the land with snow and ice. This can have devastating effects on the early arrivals because they may lack the energy reserves to survive until the thaw. At high elevations, where thick forests of spruce and fir trees are a testament to the frigid climate, the avian migrants of the boreal forest nest a month later than their low-elevation relatives.

Great Smoky Mountains National Park doesn't have spectacular jagged mountains, impressive herds of buffalo, or the largest square mileage, but the 813-square-mile park has the highest visitation rate of any national park—as many as nine million visitors annually. The hallmark of the park is its amazing biodiversity. Biologists have documented more than thirty different species of salamanders in the park, some of which are not found anywhere else in the world. More than 1,500 species of flowering plants have been found in the park, including 100 species of native trees, more than in all of northern Europe. The tumbling mountain streams of the Tennessee River drainage contain North America's most diverse group of freshwater fish—more than eighty species have been found in the park. Because of this wealth of flora and fauna, the area has been listed as an international biosphere reserve by the United Nations Educational, Scientific, and Cultural Organization's (UNESCO's) Man and the Biosphere Program.

The park's amazing diversity is due in no small part to its varied landscape. The elevation ranges from 875 feet at the park's western boundary at the mouth of Abrams Creek to the 6,643-foot peak of Clingman's Dome. Up to eighty-five inches of life-giving rain falls annually in the park, which feeds the abundant waterfalls, rushing rivers, and meandering streams.

More than anything, however, it is the opportunity to view wild animals that attracts so many visitors to Great Smoky Mountains National Park each year. Cruising along the country roads in the hopes of sighting wildlife is an iconic park activity. Lively squirrels scurry among the walnut trees along Cades Cove Loop Road, and ground hogs nibble tender grasses. Cedar waxwings, eastern blue birds, and eastern phoebes dart among the park buildings, collecting berries from nearby bushes. Chipmunks scamper about stone walls or log piles. Flocks of wild turkeys are in the meadows, gleaning seeds from the tall grasses.

Photographing animals in the wild is an exciting and rewarding challenge. In order to zoom in close to animals without disturbing their natural behaviors, we use large lenses and sturdy tripods. We know where animals are found and how they behave, and then we try to predict their actions to increase our chances of being in the right place at the right time.

Photographing baby animals is an even greater challenge as they are often hidden from predators. Patience is the greatest virtue that a wildlife photographer can learn. We have spent hours—even days—waiting for an animal to come to the water to drink when the light was right. But nothing is more thrilling when everything comes together.

Surprise is an important element of this business. You may be disappointed when the buck you want to photograph walks away. But then, when he stops, turns his head back, and stares directly into the camera as the morning sun highlights his huge rack of antlers, you know you have just captured an unforgettable image.

One of our favorite times to photograph the park's baby animals is in late summer. Black bear cubs scamper up the black cherry trees to harvest the abundant ripe fruit or to rough house, with sow nearby, keeping a watchful eye. Fawns test out their independence, one moment sallying forth and the next moment dashing back to the protection of the ever-attentive doe. The juxtaposition of a fawn with a white-tailed buck in velvet antlers is the ultimate image of the circle of life. Even before the juveniles lose their spots, the bucks grow antlers for the perennial ritual of the rut, the mating and eventual birth of a new fawn.

Born Wild in the Smokies is a book for children of all ages. We hope the images in this book will inspire you to visit this national park. And we wish you the good luck to chance upon one of nature's true miracles—the sight of a wild baby.

Above: A baby spotted skunk digs for grubs in a decaying log. Born with the ability to spray a strong compound containing foul-smelling thiols as a defense mechanism, spotted skunks spray standing on their front feet—unlike the more common striped skunk that stands on all fours to spray.

Right: This black bear cub will soon learn that the black-and-white warning coloration of a skunk sends a message: "Don't mess with me."

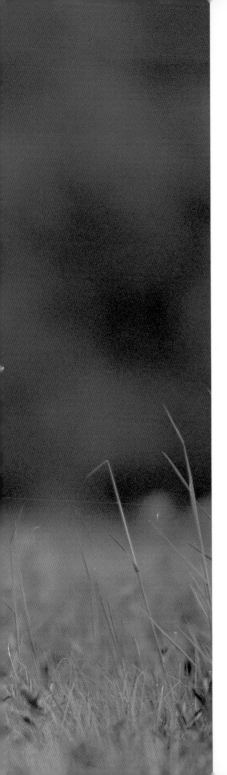

Above: A red-shouldered hawk chick stretches its wings in the nest. After a major decline in numbers the red-shouldered hawk appears to be making a comeback in the southern Appalachian Mountains.

Left: A white-tailed fawn peers out from behind its mother. In Great Smoky Mountains National Park, deer and other wild animals can be seen in areas such as Cades Cove and in the campgrounds. Observe all animals at a distance, and remember that if an animal changes its behavior because of your presence, you are too close.

Above: Eastern chipmunks are born in leaf-lined burrows one to two feet below ground. They leave their nests one month after birth and reach full size two months later.

Right: When the Tennessee shiner on the right matures, it will acquire the adult male's orange side stripe and orange mouth. Native to the Appalachians, the Tennessee shiner is a minnow that takes as long as two years to mature.

Above: Although raccoons spend most of their time on the ground, they are excellent climbers and often seek shelter in trees. Weighing nearly two ounces at birth in the springtime, this young cub is practicing its climbing.

Left: Although rarely found in Great Smoky Mountains National Park, mallards are a common sight in the Gatlinburg area.

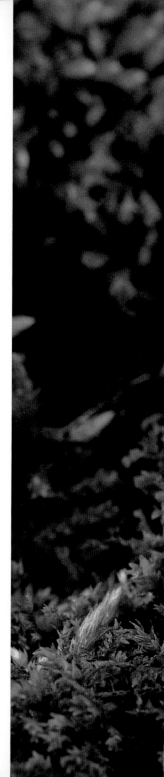

Above: Common at lower elevations in the park, the bright red male northern cardinal plays an important part in caring for the hungry cardinal chicks.

Right: The red-spotted newt goes through two distinct metamorphoses during its life. This immature red eft lives on land, which it is able to do because of the rough, protective texture of its skin, unlike the moist, delicate skin of most salamanders. In approximately two years, it will become an adult red-spotted newt that lives in the water.

Left: This wood thrush chick perches on the edge of its nest in Great Smoky Mountains National Park. Most wood thrush nests are built in eastern hemlock trees, but since 2002, the park's hemlock trees have been under attack by an insect called the hemlock woolly adelgid. No one knows what will happen to wood thrushes if these insects destroy the vast stands of hemlocks.

Facing page: A newborn fawn steps over grass wet with morning dew. Shortly after they are born, fawns are able to follow after the does.

Above: A striped skunk searches a log for insects and larvae, favored treats.

Right: A black bear cub walks along one of the 800 miles of hiking trails in the park. During the first year of its life, a cub stays with its mother while the sow teaches it the survival skills necessary to survive in the wild. Never feed or approach any bear, especially a cub.

Above: Just outside its tree cavity nest, a screech owlet tries out its developing wings. The three color morphs of the eastern screech owl and owlets are gray, red, and brown.

Left: Although they are common, bobcats are nocturnal and rarely seen in Great Smoky Mountains National Park. A litter of one to five kittens is born in April or May.

Above: In mid-summer, northern fence lizard hatchlings emerge from eggs laid under rocks or rotting logs. The adult male on the left can be distinguished from the juvenile by the blue patch on his throat. Lizards eat a wide variety of insects, including spiders, snails, beetles, and grasshoppers.

Right: This white-tailed fawn gives a sidelong glance with its large brown eyes.

Far right: Elk have an exceptional sense of smell and this elk calf is learning to detect scents in the air in order to identify predators by smell before they can be seen. The fancy collar around its neck has a radio attached so biologists can track its movements in the park. After being totally eliminated in the late 1800s by unregulated hunting and loss of habitat, elk were reintroduced to the park in 2001.

Above: The bright red color of the red eft is a warning sign to predators—it is extremely poisonous. Under attack, the red eft vigorously wiggles the tip of its wormlike tail until the predator bites it and gets a nasty toxin in its mouth. The salamander simply walks away and will eventually grow a new tail.

Left: A painted turtle climbs out of its pond to sun itself on a log, which helps eliminate irritating leeches.

Above: Eastern gray squirrels use their bushy tails to help them keep warm. During the cool mountain nights, squirrels insulate themselves by wrapping their fluffy tail around their face and body.

Facing page: This doe keeps its fawn extra clean by licking it, which also reduces odors that might attract predators. During the first month of a fawn's life, a doe hides the fawn in vegetation and returns to nurse it several times a day.

Left: Great horned owlets, such as this one, hatch as early as February. This owlet's downy feathers will keep it warm until the spring thaw.

Facing page: A black bear cub lounges in a snag. Black bear cubs are excellent tree climbers and often sleep securely nestled in the branches of a tree.

Above: In spring, neotropical migrant birds, such as this prairie warbler, fly north from tropical climates to nest in the insect-rich regions of the temperate zone. They can be found near Great Smoky Mountains National Park in areas where cedars and young pines grow.

Right: A white-tailed fawn walks through a meadow filled with early summer wildflowers. By the time a fawn is six weeks old, it relies less on the doe's milk and begins to eat a variety of succulent vegetation and grasses.

Above: Black snakes are quite common in the southern Appalachians but a two-headed snake of any variety is quite a rarity. These unusual mutations usually limit the organism's ability to survive in the wild.

Left: Young red-tailed hawks, called eyas, nest in tall trees, and occasionally strong winds or rival siblings knock a baby from the nest. If they haven't developed flight feathers, like this unfortunate chick, they will have a difficult time surviving in the wild. If you happen to find such a baby bird, do not pick it up. Contact a park ranger immediately.

Above: Named for a character in Greek mythology, the io moth caterpillar is armed with a coat of poisonous spines to ward off predators. The adult io moth has two large hidden eye spots on its hind wings. When disturbed, the moth exposes the eye spots to frighten the predator away.

Facing page: A red fox kit scratches itself, trying to rid itself of pesky fleas. Like many mammals, foxes have problems with insect pests and can sometimes be seen rolling in the dust to rid themselves of the parasites.

Right: Baby black bears lick up sweet juices from berries that have fallen on the road. The black cherry trees along the Cades Cove Loop Road provide these bears with a nutritious meal as they fatten up for the cold winter months. Park visitors have a good chance of spotting black bears in late summer and early fall.

Below: River otters are one of the park's most playful and curious animals. Because of uncontrolled trapping for their pelts, river otters had not been seen in the park since 1931. In 1986, the National Park Service began a successful reintroduction program and today otters can be found in many areas of the park, including Little River, Cataloochee Creek, and Oconaluftee River.

Above: A Canada gosling stretches its wings, practicing for its first flight.

Left: Although it looks as if raccoons are meticulously washing their food, they are actually kneading it underwater to soften it and remove any inedible parts. Raccoons have nimble front paws and can easily open picnic baskets and garbage cans.

Above: A great horned owlet is starting to show "horns" that aren't really horns at all but simply tufts of feathers. Owls are nocturnal and prey upon mammals such as skunks, rabbits, and rodents.

Right: A blue-tailed skink hatchling has distinctive yellow lines on its black body and a bright blue tail. If it is attacked by a predator, its tail will break off and continue twitching, which distracts the predator while the skink runs for cover. The tail will grow back over time.

Above: From its dome-shaped nest, a Carolina wren chick begs for food. Carolina wrens build nests in a variety of places, including stumps, stone walls, and tangled vines, and in non-natural sites such as mailboxes or tin cans.

Facing page: In their nest on the ground, these killdeer chicks are just hatching from their well-camouflaged eggs. The chicks are precocial, which means that they are capable of moving about when they are hatched and will walk away from the nest in a matter of hours.

Above: Born hairless, eastern cottontail rabbit kits begin their lives in a soft nest in the ground. They grow very fast and after about two weeks are able to leave the nest and start feeding on their own.

Facing page: Black bear cubs spend a great deal of time playing, wrestling, jostling, and rough-housing—antics that will help prepare them for the serious side of being the park's largest predator. Cubs remain under the protective care of the sow until they are about one-and-a-half years old and capable of living on their own.

Above: Robin chicks leave the nest after approximately two weeks and remain on the ground, begging for food from their parents. The young robins reach their adult size at the age of one month and are capable of flying. If you happen to find a baby robin on the ground, leave it there—the parents are likely close by.

Left: As its name suggests, the milkweed tiger moth caterpillar feeds on milkweed in the late summer. If disturbed, it rolls into a ball and drops to the ground to escape.

Above: This young green heron stands amid the rushes. Green herons hunt for fish or small invertebrates, such as water bugs, dragonflies, and crayfish, along the muddy edges of ponds and lakes.

Right: The gender of an eastern box turtle hatchling depends on the ground temperature of the nest. Eggs that are kept at cooler temperatures tend to become male turtles, and those kept at a warmer temperature tend to become female. As with tree rings, the age of a turtle can be determined by counting the rings on its scales. The carapace, or top of its shell, is composed of many ringed scales called scutes. A turtle gets a new ring added to its scales each year.

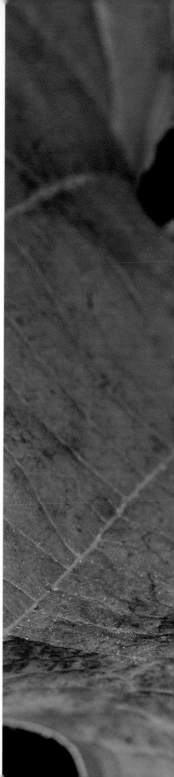

Above: Muskrats live near streams and rivers and eat the roots of underwater plants. They can remain underwater for up to fifteen minutes and eat nearly one-third of their body weight every day. Baby muskrats can swim when they are two weeks old and are fully independent at one month.

Left: Spotted dusky salamanders lay their eggs in a moist area and guard them until the babies hatch. If you look closely, you can see the developing young salamanders in the eggs. Known as the salamander capital of the world, Great Smoky Mountains National Park is home to more than thirty different species of salamanders.

Above: A southern flying squirrel peers out of a tree cavity. Southern flying squirrels don't actually fly but instead glide from tree to tree, with the flap of skin between their front and back legs acting like a sail. Although rarely seen, this nocturnal squirrel may be the most common type of squirrel in a deciduous forest.

Right: A white-tailed fawn has spots so that it is harder for a predator to see. Deer have an excellent sense of hearing and their large ears help pick up the sounds around them.

Above: This black bear cub, perched in a tree, is one of more than 1,600 bears in Great Smoky Mountains National Park—statistically two bears for every square mile of the park. Black bears are especially common in Cades Cove and Cataloochee Valley.

Left: Ruffed grouse chicks venture out from the safety of their mother's wings. When alarmed, a ruffed grouse hen holds out her wings like a protective umbrella.

Above: Watching wildlife is an exciting activity for a family visiting Cataloochee Valley. Early in the morning and late in the afternoon, herds of elk with their frolicking calves come out to feed in the lush meadows.

Right: In June, elk calves are born with spots to aid in camouflage; the spots disappear by the fall. Elk can weigh up to 700 pounds and are the largest mammal in the park. These baby elk have yet to receive the special radio collars that researchers use to study this reintroduced species.

Above: A black bear sow and her two cubs peek through the brush. Most bears are shy around humans but can become a nuisance if fed. If bears become a nuisance, they have to be relocated and thus have a smaller chance of survival than those that remain in their home territory.

Left: With a life span of nearly twenty years, the beaver is the largest North American rodent, weighing up to seventy pounds. In the eighteenth and nineteenth centuries, American beavers were heavily trapped for their pelts and their numbers significantly declined.

Above: This fawn curls up in the grass while its mother grazes nearby—always within hearing distance. A fawn's ability to remain motionless helps keep predators from finding it in the meadows and thickets.

Right: A red fox kit strolls through a field as the setting sun warms its fuzzy fur.

Above: The obviously round pupils of this black snake hatchling are an indication that it is nonvenomous. Immediately after birth, this hatchling will be ready to hunt insects without the aid of any parent. Black snakes are important members of the food chain that help to keep the rodent populations down.

Left: Reptiles, such as this black snake hatchling, push their way through their tough leathery eggs. Black snake hatchlings have a blotchy pattern when they are young, which is the source of a common, but erroneous, notion that black snakes cross breed with copperhead snakes.

Above: A barn swallow feeds two hungry chicks a tasty insect. Their mud nests can often be found under the eves of buildings around the park, in the campgrounds and in Cades Cove.

Right: Red bats nurse their young until they are five weeks old and able to fend for themselves. While flying, bats capture insects, such as moths, and thereby play an important role in controlling insect populations.

© MERLIN D. TUTTLE, BAT CONSERVATION INTERNATIONAL, INC.

Facing page: With its large eyes that enable it to see at night, this great horned owlet can hunt by itself at one to two months of age. The great horned owl is found only at lower elevations, but the more common black-eyed barred owl can be found throughout the park.

Above: Once frequently seen in the park's open areas, the numbers of northern bobwhites have dropped in the park and in all of the Appalachian Mountains in recent years. Biologists are trying to determine the reason for the decrease in numbers.

Left: Eastern cottontail rabbits can be found in brushy areas and along roadsides throughout the park. The Appalachian cottontail rabbit, which lives in the park's densely forested areas such as Low Gap and Pine Knot Branch, is similar but more rarely observed.

Above: A black bear cub climbs in a white oak tree along Cades Cove Loop Road. Black bears are omnivores and eat a wide variety of foods, including berries, nuts, insects, and carrion. Bears are very intelligent and will try to scavenge food from campsites or garbage cans.

Right: Imitator salamanders live in the park's higher elevations, such as Clingman's Dome, Newfound Gap, and on a few nearby peaks. This young salamander lacks the red cheek patches that characterize adults. These unique cheek patches mimic those of the red-cheeked salamander, another of the park's endemic inhabitants.

Above: A turkey vulture chick is silhouetted against the weather-beaten wall of an old building. Turkey vultures nest in hollow logs, caves, or even abandoned buildings. With their acute sense of smell, they find carrion from miles away and are an important part of the food chain because they clean up the remains of deceased animals.

Left: A colony of albino groundhogs is well known near the Oconaluftee Visitor Center. This young groundhog pokes its head above the grass, ever mindful of the red-tailed hawk nearby.

71

Above: This American kestrel chick is a type of falcon. They are often seen hunting from tree snags and telephone wires in open areas, especially along the edges of the park.

Right: Dish-faced and fuzzy, these three barn owlets belong to a species that was once found in the park; recent attempts to reintroduce them have been unsuccessful. If you happen to see a large, white, ghost-like owl at night please report it to a park ranger.

Above: Brook trout are native to the cool, fast-flowing waters of the Great Smoky Mountains. This baby brook trout has vertical black lines shaped like thumbprints—called parr marks—that help to conceal it from predators.

Facing page: The aim of the reintroduction program is to establish a stable population of elk in Great Smoky Mountains National Park. Elk cows give birth to one calf a year, with a lifespan of nearly fifteen years.

Above: Although this Virginia opossum joey may resemble a large rat, it is actually related to a kangaroo—and is the only marsupial in North America. Baby opossums are born only twelve to thirteen days after conception, then they mature for two months in a fur-lined pouch on their mother's abdomen—the shortest gestation period of any North American mammal. Opossums are scavengers and play an important part in the ecosystem by eating some foods that other animals may not, such as decomposing garbage and carrion. When threatened, they play dead, which inspired the expression "playing possum."

Right: The white-footed mouse, along with its close relative the deer mouse, is one of the most abundant mammals in the park. Females produce two to four litters of babies a year.

Far right: The fluffy feathers of this baby eastern screech owl help to protect it from the colder temperatures of early spring.

Left: This pileated woodpecker brings food to its chicks, housed in a hole that it has hammered into a tree trunk. The babies will soon be old enough to fledge from the nest to find their own food. Carpenter ants are the favored food of the largest woodpecker in the park.

Facing page: This painted turtle hatchling, with its bright shell and stout legs, explores the ponds and streams in Cades Cove. When the four to fifteen turtles hatch out of their underground nest, they can immediately fend for themselves.

Rob Simpson is a professor of natural resources and the head of the nature and outdoor photography program at Lord Fairfax Community College in Virginia, teaching courses in field biology and nature photography. Born in Canada, Rob has worked as a park naturalist in Ontario's Rondeau Provincial Park, as an environmental inventory scientist locating rare and endangered plants and animals for the Department of Natural Resources, and as a field research scientist for the Canadian Wildlife Service. He has discovered two new plant taxa, which were named after him—*Spiranthes x simpsonii* and *Dryosticum x simpsonii*.

Ann Simpson is a professor of anatomy and physiology, and chairs the science department at Lord Fairfax Community College. She co-teaches nature photography classes with Rob and organizes the international nature photography and natural history tours that she and Rob lead to countries including Africa, Canada, Costa Rica, Ecuador, the Galapagos Islands, Trinidad, and Tobago.

The Simpsons' expertise as professional biologists gives their photography an in-depth style. As owners of Simpson's Nature Photography, they specialize in photographing species that are difficult to find. Their images have appeared in publications including *National Geographic, National Parks, National Geographic KIDS, American Park Network Guides,* and *Virginia Wildlife,* and on the covers of publications for Defenders of Wildlife, National Wildlife, and the Nature Conservancy. They have published work in Audubon Field Guides, Kaufman Field Guides, and *Birds of Shenandoah.* Their work can be seen at www.agpix.com/snphotos